Always dream BIG!

♡ Nicole
Onwuason

Little Peanut's
BIG DREAMS

By
Nicole Onwuasor

Illustrated by
Joe Figueroa

What do I want to be when I grow up? My mom and dad said I could be anything I want to be.

I want to be a dancer.

I want to be an actor.

I want to be a teacher.

I want to be an athlete.

I want to be a fire fighter.

I want to be a police officer.

I want to be a pilot.

I want to be an astronaut.

I want to be a veterinarian.

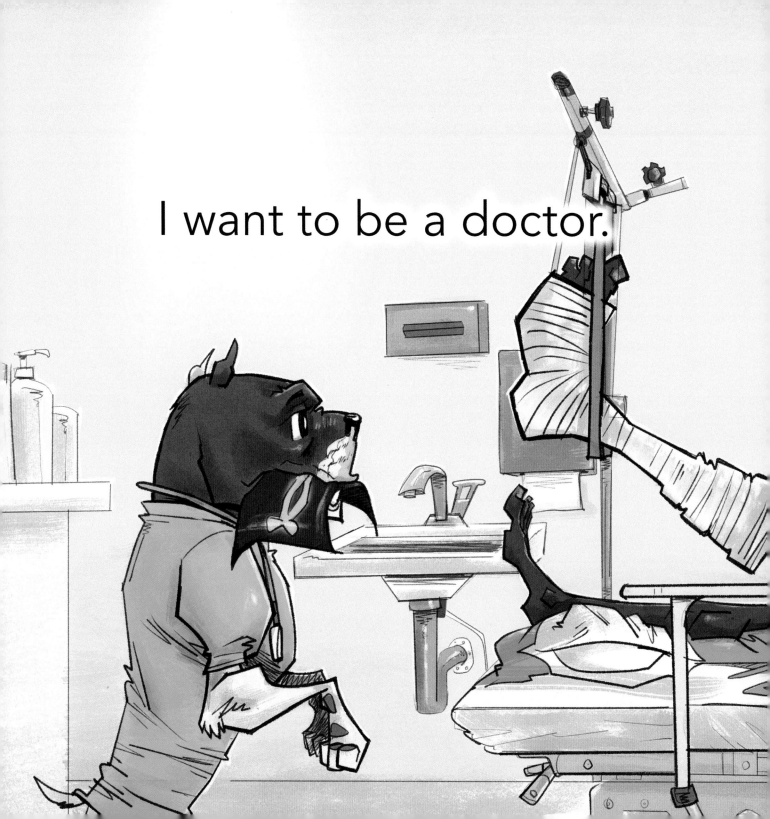

What do I want to be when I grow up? I have so many choices! My mom and dad were right. I can be anything I want to be!

Bio:

Nicole Onwuasor is a born and raised Oregonian now living in Arizona with her family. She is a wife and a mom of two playful boys and two slobbery fur babies. She received her Bachelor of Science in Geography from Portland State University in 2016 and her Master's degree in Special Education from George Fox University in 2017. Teaching in special education solidified her passion for teaching and love of inclusivity. Nicole loves to spend time outdoors with her family, traveling, and planning her next girl's night.

www.nicoleonwuasor.com

Made in the USA
Monee, IL
08 June 2023

35165041R00024